POTTY-MOUTHED

POTTY-MOUTHED

Big Thoughts from Little Brains

ANNE JOHNSOS with drawings by John Britton

SPARKPRESS

Published by SparkPress, a BookSparks imprint,
A division of SparkPoint Studio, LLC
Tempe, Arizona, USA, 85281
www.gosparkpress.com

Published 2017
Printed in Canada
Print ISBN: 978-1-943006-30-4
E-SBN: 978-1-943006-31-1

Library of Congress Control Number: 2017955185

Cover and interior design by Tabitha Lahr
Illustrations by John Britton

For Clark, Sof-a-lof, Banana, Baba, and Boots.

Thanks for teaching me to love and be loved
with humor, grace, and gratitude.

iNTRODUCTiON:

Before I became a parent, I was "judgy." I watched harried moms and dads and their misbehaving small ones, thinking, "I would never use 'baby talk.'"

Or "Why can't they control what their children say?"

And "Is anyone going to wipe that kid's nose?"

Then I had my children.

Every day of motherhood has offered various combinations of trials, triumphs, delight, despair, comedy, drama, joy, pain, frustration and deep pride.

It has been better than cable.

Now I am the mother I used to judge. At a black-tie affair I inadvertently ask, "Where's the potty?"

I call noodles "noo-noos" and water "wah-wah" and the Baby Mozart CD we play at bedtime "doot doots."

When out to dinner on a rare "date night," I find myself cutting my steak into tiny pieces before taking a bite . . . or, worse yet, reaching over to cut my husband's steak for him.

Without flinching I extend my hand to hold a wad of gum or something extracted from a nostril.

And almost daily I am left with my mouth hanging open after hearing the thoughts and words that escape my children's mouths.

For several years I've been writing down our conversations, secretly typing notes on my phone so I could record them verbatim. (Note: The kids have had their share of speech impediments. If you see a "w" or "y" that doesn't appear to belong, try replacing it with an "r" or "l." Many times it was my inability to understand that made the exchanges humorous.)

This is the first in a series of books comprising the stolen moments and lessons learned as my children discovered the language of life.

ROMANCE:

Sitting on the deck with Husband.
Drinking wine.

Listening to Mozart . . .

. . . AS IT PLAYS THROUGH
THE BABY MONITOR

LIGHT READING:

Just went to tidy 4-year-old's room and found book titled "CPR for Family and Friends" in said child's bed.

Not sure whether to be alarmed or relieved.

BiRTH ORDER:

4-year-old (from the back seat): *Mommy, when aww duh peopwe die, wiww duh eahwf be destwoyed?*

2-year-old: *I want mohw fwies! (with one sticking out of her nose)*

SURPRISE:

Was looking intently at the little face of the 2-year-old, thinking about the love a parent has for a child. Then the 2-year-old leaned over and licked me.
"I puppy!" she shrieked.

Another developmental milestone.

4-YEAR-OLD HUMOR:

Teach 2-year-old sister to shout "I stupid" when she gets mad.

Then make her mad again and again . . .
And again.

NATURE OR NURTURE?

The 2-year-old keeps running headfirst into the couch, bouncing off and saying "scoose me."

CAREER STRATEGIES:

Me (to 4-year-old): *What do you want to be when you grow up?*

4-year-old: *A Indian.*

Me: *(pause) Why?*

4-year-old: *Because dehwe awen't dat many yeft.*

MEALTiME FAiL:

Something I thought I would never say: "No, you may not leave the table. Not until you take two more bites of your hot dog."

BODiLY FLUiDS:

The 2-year-old has discovered the "farmer's blow" and uses it often.

Please, head cold, end soon.

CLEAN FLOORS:

Just realized why I love vacuuming:

I enjoy the peace and quiet.

ANOTHER MEALTIME FAIL:

Would like to thank McDonald's for making all other meals "unhappy" in the eyes of my 5-year-old.

SLEEP TRAINING:

2-year-old (standing by her parents' bed at 6 a.m. every day since foolish parents moved her out of the crib and into a "big girl" bed): *It's sunny time!*

Is it wrong to lock a child in her room?

PUMPKIN FARM:

5-year-old (while being held over a public toilet in 90-degree weather): *I yub you mohw dan duh twinkwes in duh staws.*

Worth it.

NEGOTIATIONS:

2-year-old (at 7:30 a.m., referring to Halloween candy still in plastic pumpkin on top shelf of cabinet): *Mama, I hab a punkin tweat?*

Me: *No, baby. Not until after lunch.*

2-year-old: *Mama, I hab yunch?*

"POTTY" WORDS:

2-year-old (after being asked to list all the bad words she knows . . . because she was throwing them around willy nilly):

Poop, peeps, diawwhea, tuwd, (and here's where it gets interesting . . .) *eyebaww, and mustasse.*

We told her never ever to say mustache again.

BATH-TIME DELIGHTS:

Is recovering from a bathtime not unlike the pool scene from *Caddyshack*.

But it wasn't a Baby Ruth.

CLEAN SLATE:

5-year-old (to her sister on the eve of the first day of kindergarten): *Tomowwohw my new yife begins.*

Let's hope her past doesn't catch up with her.

POWER OF PRAYER:

3-year-old (after being told she could not have another "treat"):

(sigh)

Deaw God, would you yike me to have anuddew tweat?

(pause)

Him said 'yes.'

PARENTING PRIVILEGE:

5-year-old: *Mama, I'm sowwy when I yeww at my sistuhw. It's dust dat I want to be mohwe yike you.*

Me (in my head): *Touché, small grownup.*

Me (out loud): *You're not her mother. When YOU are a mother, you can yell, too.*

DEFLECTiON:

2-year-old passes gas in the loudest way imaginable and then looks behind her.

Me: *What are you looking for?*

2-year-old: *Daddy.*

iYUCK:

"This accessory is not made to work with iPhone."
(The message that appears when one's 2-year-old
sticks one's iPhone into her oatmeal.)

SQUISHY MOMMY:

5-year-old (after a bout of roughhousing with her dad): *Mommy, I want to sit by you.*

Me (touched): *You want some snuggles?*

5-year-old: *No. I dust want a softhouse.*

KiLLER FRUiT:

5-year-old: *Next yeaw can we get duh Gween Gwapehw fohw ouw Hayyoween decowations?*

Me: *(pause) The Green Graper?*

5-year-old: *Yeah. Duh guy who comes tuh get you when it's time to be dead.*

LULLABY:

5-year-old: *If dat song is for weaw, I bet a yotta yittuhwl guhwls hope duh mockingbuhwd won't sing.*

Me: *And some big girls, too.*

EXTRACTION:

More words I thought I'd never say: *"Hey, you have a big booger in there. Let me get it out for you."*

"STAYING ALIVE":

Me (speaking to girls in back seat during long car ride): *We'd get there faster if you took a power nap.*

5-year-old: *What's a powehw nap?*

Me: *A short nap that makes you feel better.*

5-year-old: *Ooooooohhh. You mean a disco nap.*

SILVER LINING?:

5-year-old: *Who was King Midas?*

Me: *Someone who could touch something and turn it to gold.*

5-year-old: *What's gohwd?*

Me: *Money.*

5-year-old: *So if you touched me and tuwned me to money, would you be sad?*

Me: *Yes. (pause) And then I'd spend you.*

NOT BAD
FOR A STEPDAD:

Went to straighten up the crèche and found Joseph nestled between Ariel and Sleeping Beauty.

EVERYONE HAS A TALENT:

Me (texting from test site for public-school gifted program): *Every other 5-year-old here is reading out loud. Ours is watching YouTube clips about Scooby.*

Husband (texting back): *I'll bet those other kids can't fart on command.*

And that is why I married him.

SPEECH THERAPY CAN'T HAPPEN SOON ENOUGH:

5-year-old (outside church this evening):
Mommy, when I gohw up wiww I get bwests?

Me: *Um.* (blink blink) *Well, yes. Most girls do.*

Husband: *She asked if she would get BLESSED.*

EVERYONE'S A CRITIC:

5-year-old: *Mommy, why don't you weaw makeup when you dwive me to schoow?*

Me: *Why? I'm just dropping you off. I don't even get out of the car.*

5-year-old: *Duh caw has windows.*

REBRANDING?:

The 3-year-old has been asking for weeks if she can see some "spooky rocks." I have pointed out every rock we have seen, but 3-year-old has not been satisfied. Then we drove by a cemetery. 3-year-old screamed "Dehwe dem awh! Spooky wocks!"

Tombstones.

WORST SNICKERS COMMERCIAL EVER:

3-year-old (while sitting on potty): *Mama, I need hehwp.*

Me (kneeling in front of her): *That's OK. I'm here.*

3-year-old (putting arms around my neck and head on my shoulder): *Dis couwd take a whiwe.*

It did.

PINT-SIZED WISDOM:

3-year-old: *Food makes you big and stwong.*
Wine makes you a happy famiwy.

Um.

MAKING A POINT:

5-year-old (after being told quietly but firmly to stop teasing her sister): *Why do you always yeww at me?*

Me: *That was not yelling. THIS IS YELLING!*

(Stunned silence . . . followed by peals of laughter)

3-year-old: *Do dat again!*

Point made. Sort of.

MARBLES:

Me: *What's in your mouth?*

3-year-old: *A choking hazuhwd.*

At least she was honest.

CiTY LiFE:

3-year-old (seeing a shiny Trojan Magnum wrapper on the sidewalk): *Was dat a spessuwhl tweat?*

Me: *(pause) I suspect it was for *someone.*

RETAIL TODDLER:

3-year-old (after being handed a fortune cookie with the fortune peeking out from its baked cocoon): *Mama, can you take duh tag off 'dis?*

HARD TRUTH:

5-year-old: *Daddy is the Tweat Man!*

3-year-old: *And duh Fahwt Man!*

Me: *What is Mommy then?*

5-year-old: *Duh cweaning woman.*

EVEN MORE BODILY FLUIDS:

3-year-old (after trying to get to Grandma's bathroom and negotiate party tights): *I'm yeaking!*

(Insert mad dash by both parents and frenzied mopping plus costume change)

3-year-old: *Thanks fohw fixing duh yeak.*

FiRST SNiFF iS FREE:

I think Windex might be a gateway drug. Every time I clean the kitchen, the 5-year-old sneaks in to sniff the countertops.

GUT PUNCH:

5-year-old (as I wake her when I get home from late night at work): *Mommy, why do you yeave me so much?*

Me: *I'm sorry, but tomorrow I'll be there when you wake up.*

5-year-old: *Will you take a showehw fuhwst?*

READY FOR HER CLOSEUP:

5-year-old (after dancing in rec room and then realizing I am paying attention to 3-year-old, who is cutting herself with scissors): *Awe you wattsing me?*

Me: *Yes. Sorry. Go ahead and dance.*

5-year-old: *I don't want to dance if no one is wattsing.*

TRAINING:

5-year-old (while trying to play "princesses" with me and finding me unable to sound exactly like a princess): (*sigh*) *It's hahwd to twain a mommy.*

MORE LIGHT READING:

Found 3-year-old "reading" to her little stuffed piggies this morning.

Book title: *Heart of Darkness*.

TROUBLE:

3-year-old (after donning princess dress, crown and flower hair clip): *I wish dehwe wewe boys hehwe.*

Me: *Why?*

3-year-old: *So we can dance.*

Me: *You can dance with me.*

3-year-old: *I ohn-yee dance wif boys, siwwy.*

STYLIN' SKIN:

3-year-old: *Why don't I have pohka dots?*

Me: *Huh? Who has polka dots?*

3-year-old: *Mama.* (Crosses room, approaches me and sticks small finger into mole on my face)

3-year-old: *See? Pohka dot!*

GENDERS EXPLAINED:

Me: *What's the difference between boys and girls?*

5-year-old: *Guhws have puwr-ses.*

3-year-old: *Guhws have makeup.*

5-year-old: *Guhws have fancy boots.*

3-year-old: *Guhws don't have mustass-es.*

If they're lucky.

ESTATE PLANNING:

3-year-old: *Mama, when wiww you be died?*

Me: *What??*

3-year-old: *Daddy says evewybody gets died.*

Me: *Oh! Well, let's not worry about that.*
Let's live every minute and be happy.
Let's love our lives. Don't worry, honey.

3-year-old: *(pause) When you*
get died, can I have youw neckwace?

AGED TO PERFECTION:

5-year-old: *Waisins awe yike gwandma gwapes.*

Me: *Why?*

5-year-old: *Duh winkuhws.*

GEOGRAPHY:

3-year-old (working on a puzzle of the United States): *Dehwe's duh Stat-sue of Yibya!*

Um.

LADIES' CHOICE:

5-year-old (as I approach to help her ride her bike):
Mama, stay whewe you awe. You know a yady needs hehw pwivacy.

Me (stopping short): *What?*

5-year-old: *You didn't expect a 5-yeaw-ohd to say dat, did you?*

Nope.

HONESTY:

3-year-old (upon seeing me after a dramatic haircut): *Mama, you get a haiwcut?*

Me: *Yes.*

3-year-old bursts into tears.

Me: *What's wrong?*

3-year-old: *Now we not matching.*

Me: *That's OK. Do you want to get YOUR hair cut?*

3-year-old: *No.*

(But it sounded like "HELL, no.")

HOLY CRACKERS:

3-year-old (peering into backpack while on vacation last week): *I found Cheezis!*

Me: *You found Cheezits?*

3-year-old: *No.* (Then she inexplicably pulls a crucifix from the backpack.) *I found Chesus!*

Does this mean she's been saved?

WHITE LIES:

Husband (as 5-year-old applies shockingly odoriferous hand lotion given to her by a great aunt): *It smells like a New York strip club in here.*

5-year-old: *What's a stwip cwub?*

(Silence while I glare at Husband.)

Me: *It's a place where they serve steak. New York strip steak.*

Thank goodness he didn't say "a Bangkok whorehouse."

MOMMY MAKEOVER:

5-year-old (tentatively, after handing me a handmade invitation for a Mother's Day event at school):
Do you have to wohwk that day?

Me: *No! I'll be there!*

5-year-old: *Good. Weaw something weal, weal, weal, weal pwetty.* (She points at my jeans and polo.) *Not yike dat.*

TODDLERS ARE LITERAL:

3-year-old: *I made somessing for you fohw Mudduhws's Day.*

Me: *Oooooh. I can't wait!*

3-year-old: *It's a neckwace.*

WHISKERS:

Husband often rubs his chin against the girls' cheeks, a phenomenon known as "whisker rubs." The girls scream with laughter, making me wish I could cause similar delight.

Me: *Mommy wishes she could give whisker rubs, but she doesn't have any whiskers.*

3-year-old: *Yes hehw does. Hehw has whiskehws on hehw yegs.*

So much for not shaving as often during the winter.

MOMMY iS:

6-year-old's classmate (at Mother's Day event):
My mommy is special because she makes me cookies.

Another classmate: *My mommy is special because she cooks me dinner.*

Another: *My mommy is special because she knits me sweaters. (I start to sweat.)*

My 6-year-old: *My mommy is special . . . because she is funny. #epicrelief #justalittlebitofpride*

PROBABLE CAUSE:

3-year-old: *Mama, Piggy have markehw on him.*

Me: *How did that happen?*

3-year-old: *Pwowwy I dwawed on him.*

Me: *Probably?*

3-year-old: *Den pwowwy I twied to wipe it off. And pwowwy it didn't wohwk.*

Me: *Probably.*

TiME FOR A NEW SiTTER:

3-year-old (during the instrumental interlude in "Copacabana"): *Mohwe cowbeww!*

#hasshebeenwatchingSNL?

SOME JOKES AREN'T FUNNY:

3-year-old (as her dad goes into bathroom to shave):

Pwowwy him needs his piwacy.

Me: *Arrrrrrrrrrrrrrrrr, matey.*

3-year-old cocks head, blinks and says nothing.

PROFESSIONALLY SPEAKING:

3-year-old: *I cute because I yittuhw.*

6-year-old: *That's because all little people awe cute.*

Me: *Right. When you're little, you're cute. As you get older, you become beautiful.*

6-year-old: *And when you get way old like Mama, you get pwofessional.*

MORE BATH-TIME DELIGHTS:

Overheard while girls were playing in the bath (pretending foam letters were characters in some sort of drama):

6-year-old: *Mawk my words. I'll be back.*

3-year-old: *We sall see about dat, Muchacho.*

#si

CLEANiNG:

3-year-old (referring to the people who sometimes come help after birthdays, baptisms and barbecues): *When is da cweanehws coming?*

Me: *I'm not sure. Why?*

3-year-old: *Dis pwace is a mess.*

This from the walking, talking shedder of crumbs, clothes and the occasional bodily fluid.

DYSON VERSUS DISNEY:

Pretty sure I just vacuumed Cinderella's slipper.

#lookslikeshe'llstayamaid

MORE CLEANING:

I am so pleased when 3-year-old tries to "help" by "cleaning." Until I find the 3-year-old "cleaning" the bathroom walls with . . . THE TOILET BRUSH.

(Yes, it was right after she "cleaned" the toilet.)

DOG DAYS:

The 3-year-old has an alter ego named "Cookie."
It's a puppy. It wears a furry vest (even in 100-degree
weather) but will not wear pants. It speaks its own
language, pees on the floor and generally drives the
rest of the family crazy. I used to try to stop Cookie
from emerging, but it was no use. So I decided to
play "fetch." Now I rather enjoy having a dog.

SOMETIMES:

Lyrics to the song 3-year-old made up (and sang repeatedly) as I drove the girls to swim lessons:

I yove my daddy. I yove my sistuwh. And sometimes I yove my mom.

VENTING:

Me (walking into room to find 3-year-old sticking ribbons INTO AN OUTLET): *NOOOOOOOO! No! No! No!*

3-year-old: *Why not? Dey'we not my body parts. Dey'we just wibbons.*

Me (picking up 3-year-old and holding her like a baby): *They can catch fire and hurt you. Never stick anything in an outlet. Here. See this vent on the floor? You can stick the ribbons in here.*

3-year-old: *But dat's my piggy bank.*

Sure enough. Loads of spare change in a vent that's glued shut.

Worth every penny.

UNHAPPY ENDINGS:

Is reminded of the story "Harold and the Purple Crayon." Except THIS story would be called "3-Year-Old and the Sharpie," and its ending is not quite as happy.

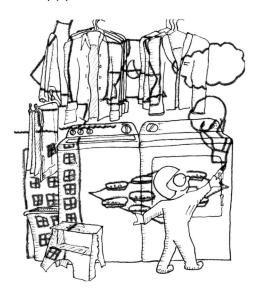

BEAUTY SECRET:

6-year-old: *Why awe they called beauty mawks when they awen't beautiful?*

Me: *But they ARE beautiful. Your beauty mark makes you look different from other people, and that makes you YOU. If we all looked the same, how beautiful would anyone be?*

3-year-old: *Does I have a cutie mawk?*

Me: *Not yet, but a few years in the sun will change that.*

6-year-old: *You have a LOT.*

Me: *That must mean I'm very beautiful.*

(Complete and utter silence from the back seat of the car.)

VOLCABULARY LESSONS:

Me (while driving with family up a historic but dilapidated avenue): *I love this stretch and its history.*

Husband: *Maybe you'd like to stay at a hot sheets motel.*

6-year-old (in back seat): *What's a hot sheets motel?*

Me (mumbling): *It's a place where the sheets are warm because, er . . .*

Husband: *They keep washing them and taking them out of the dryer.*

6-year-old: *Oooh. I weal want to stay at a hot sheets motel.*

3-year-old: *HOT SSEETS! HOT SSEETS!*

NOT LiTTLE:

3-year-old (after dumping a bottle of water on her head): *I is not a yittuhw guhw anymohw.*

I am not convinced.

WHAT'S IN A NAME?:

The 6-year-old got a new stuffed animal. A sweet little lion, which she promptly named and started to love. But every time she says the lion's name, I laugh out loud. And I fear the day when the 6-year-old brings the lion in for Show and Tell. Why, you ask? What could the name be?

"Fuzzy Balls."

SMILE AND NOD:

Was sitting with my laptop at the dining room table when a naked 3-year-old emerged from the basement, opened a kitchen cabinet, grabbed two granola bars, and retreated.

I went back to my typing.

Some questions are better left unanswered.

BATHROOM BEHAVIOR:

6-year-old (still sitting on the toilet after taking care of business): *I hit the jackpot!*

(Then she slumps over and starts fake snoring.)

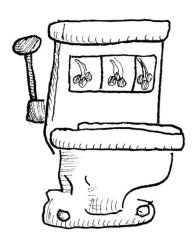

MOMMY TREAT:

3-year-old: *Tomowohw I ssink you need to be spod.*

Me: *Spod?*

6-year-old: *You know. When someone wubs youw shouldews and puts pickles on youw eyes.*

Me: *Ah. "Spa"-ed.*

CHANGING TASTES:

Me (to 3-year-old, who is a regular eater of red peppers): *Want some red peppers?*

3-year-old: *I don't yike wed peppews anymohwe.*

Me: *Since when?*

3-year-old: *Tuesday.*

Me: *Oh.*

SUPER POWERS:

3-year-old: *I took some-sing fwom youw wawwet. A cwedit cawd.*

Me: *Where is it?*

3-year-old: *I has supehw powews! I made it disapeaw.*

(Extended silence from me.)

3-year-old: *It's in my woom.*

SCiSSORS AND CENSHORSHiP:

I walk into 3-year-old's room to help with pajamas and notice an overturned shoebox top with several clumps of bright blonde hair in it.

Me (to 3-year-old): *Whose hair is this?*

3-year-old: *I don't know.*

Me (taking a deep breath): *Whose hair is this?*

3-year-old (looking furtively around the room and focusing on a stuffed animal): *Monkey's?*

Me (spying the child-safe scissors tucked behind the lamp): *Whose. Hair. Is. This????*

Then I see the side of 3-year-old's head.

The rest of this post has been censored due to adult language (in my head and almost uttered aloud).

PARENTING LESSONS:

I look up from reading a book and see 3-year-old slowly and quietly ripping pages from an aging paperback.

Me: *What are you DOING?*

3-year-old: *Nussin'.*

Me: *We don't rip books. We love books.*

3-year-old: *Sowwy.*

I pick up pieces of former book and search for cover or title page. Then I see it: *Dr. Spock's Baby and Child Care.*

HALF-TRUTH:

3-year-old: *Mommy, you fix Piggy's head?*

Me: *What happened to his head?*

3-year-old: *It got wipped.*

Me: *Wait a minute. The top of his head is missing. Where did it go?*

3-year-old: *Maybe it got cut.*

Me: *Cut . . . How?*

3-year-old: *Da scissuhws?*

JAWOHL:

6-year-old: *Daddy, I know how to say hello in German.*

Husband: *How?*

6-year-old: *Fig Newton!*

Husband: *Guten Tag?*

6-year-old: *That's what I said.*

REAPiNG:

Me (as 3-year-old wails, wanting to be carried upstairs for bedtime): *Why are you being so dramatic?*

3-year-old (stops abruptly and answers matter-o'-fact-ly): *Because Daddy's not hehwe.*

Me: *Wait. What?*

3-year-old: *Daddy's not hehwe.*

Me: *So you're not dramatic when he's around?*

3-year-old: *No. It wounnent wohwk.*

You reap what you sow.

BEAUTiFUL:

3-year-old: *Mama, does you want to be bootiful?*

Me: *Why, yes. Yes I do.*

(3-year-old climbs onto couch where I am sitting, drags fleece blanket over my head, and plops a pillow on top.)

3-year-old: *Dehwe! Bootiful!*

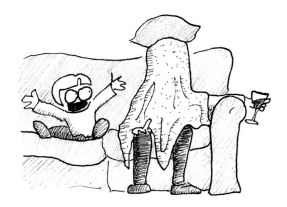

STALL TACTICS:

Me (to 4-year-old, who doesn't want to go to bed): *Pick out a story or Mommy's leaving.*

4-year-old goes to bookcase, studies shelves, and pulls out "The Giving Tree."

Me: *Oh! That's my favorite book.*

4-year-old: *Me, too.*

Me: *I like it because it shows how much you can love someone. And how good it feels to share. And how much even the littlest thing matters. Why do you like it?*

4-year-old: *It's yong.*

DARK LOGIC:

6-year-old (after confessing that she talked during a fire drill and suffered a public rebuke from a hall monitor): *Mama, do you still love me?*

Me: *Of course. I don't stop loving you when you make mistakes. In fact, I love you more and more every day.*

(Silence. And then . . .)

6-year-old: *So you didn't love me the day I was born?*

PARENT-TEACHER CONFERENCES:

6-year-old's teacher: *She is such a well-behaved child. She reads at the third-grade level. She raises her hand. She's a delight to have in class.*

4-year-old's teacher: *She could use some help taking direction. And she's awfully social. But she makes me laugh out loud. And she knows it.*

Which one will be president?

DOCTOR VISITS:

4-year-old (on way to annual checkup):
Mama, what does duh doctuhw do?

Me: *She just asks questions and makes sure you're healthy.*

4-year-old: *What's heawfy?*

Me: *Eating fruits and vegetables. NOT eating Gummi Bears.*

4-year-old: *(pause) Maybe we should keep duh Gummi Beaws a secwet.*

6-year-old: *We can't keep secwets fwom the doctuhw!*

Me (thinking back to the time time I told my doctor I drink "occasionally"): *What do you two want for dinner?*

PRAYING:

6-year-old (describing field trip to a farm with a muddy, slippery hill): *I stawted to fall and I was like, "Jesus Chwist!"*

Me: *What? We don't say that! We say His name when we talk about religion and when we pray.*

6-year-old: *(pause, and then, quietly) I WAS pwaying . . . that I didn't fall down.*

OH. THAT:

6-year-old: *Mama?*

Me: *What?*

6-year-old: *Mama?*

Me: *What?*

6-year-old: *Mama?*

Me: *(deep breath) What?*

6-year-old: *Mama?*

Me: *WHAT???*

6-year-old: *(pauses and then says quietly) I love you.*

DEFINING TIME:

4-year-old: *Mama, is today tomowwohw?*

Me: *No. Today is today. Why?*

4-year-old: *'Cause at bedtime on the day befowe today, you said Gwandma would yeave tomowwohw . . . and now ssees yeaving.*

No point in trying to describe yesterday, I suppose.

BiOLOGy:

4-year-old (seeing woman who is about a month away from having a baby): *Hew has a baby in hew bewwy.*

Me: *How do you think it got there?*

(pause)

4-year-old: *Ssee ate it?*

Me: *And how will it get out?*

6-year-old: *She'll poop it?*

Me: *That's pretty close.*

VENTRILOQUISM:

4-year-old: *I can tawk wiffout moving my yips.*

Me: *OK. Show me.*

4-year-old closes her mouth and stares quietly at me.

Me: *Are you talking?*

4-year-old nods head.

I raise one eyebrow.

4-year-old (mouth still closed): *vwwwy quwwtwy.*

THE FACE OF GOD (SORT OF):

6-year-old (from back seat): *What does God look like?*

Me: *I don't know. What do you think?*

6-year-old: *I think he looks like Jesus but bigguhw.*

4-year-old (shouting): *I ssink him weahw a gween outfit and a gween hat.*

Because God is a leprechaun.

FUTURE LOUNGE LIZARD:

For a few years now the 6-year-old, when left alone, has picked up a book, a doll, even a nickel and started serenading it. She sings, hums, clicks, squeaks, and generally sounds other-worldly. I have never interrupted or questioned the process because the grandmas say it's her way of recharging. Then tonight...

Me: *Dinner's ready!*

(Downstairs the clicks, beeps and arpeggios continue.)

Me: *Hello-o? Dinner is ready!*

(More alien noise.)

Me: *Come and eat!*

6-year-old (after a minute or two . . . emerging from the basement): *Sowwy. I was into a 'speciawwy good scat session.*

ELECTRIC PERSONALITY:

4-year-old: *Mama, I did sumssin.*

Me: *What did you do?*

4-year-old: *Duh yights.*

Me (looking into living room and seeing Christmas tree plugged in): *Oh!* (I grab the 4-year-old in a hug/vice grip.) *I love the lights, but I do not want you touching the cord. Please tell Mommy when you want them on.*

4-year-old: *It's awwight. I dinnent get ewected.*

Me (to myself): *Why do I think someday you WILL be elected?*

EVEN MORE WHITE LIES:

6-year-old: *Who was Maewy Magdawine?*

Me: *A friend of Jesus.*

4-year-old: *Wehwe dem in yuv?*

Me: *Nope. Just friends.*

6-year-old: *What did she do befowe she met Jesus?*

Me (pausing and then): *She was in "sales."*

GLAD:

6-year-old (after waking up, complaining that her leg hurt and asking for help putting on her jeans): *My leg is my enemy.*

Me (kneeling in front of her and pushing the jeans up the offending limb): *You probably just slept on it the wrong way.*

6-year-old: *Will the pain last fowevewh?*

Me: *Just a day or two.*

6-year-old: *Then I suppose you''' have to keep dwessing me. Like a baby. An itty, bitty baby.*

(Silence.)

6-year-old: *Awen't you glad I'm not always this dwamatic?*

CHILDPROOFING:

4-year-old (entering the room with a Sharpie in one chubby little fist and a bottle of car touch-up paint in the other): *It is awwwight dat I has dese?*

Husband: *Let me get you some poison to play with, too.*

OLiVER TWiST?:

The 4-year-old likes to sneak up behind her daddy, reach into his back pocket, pull out his wallet and then run away, yelling, "Stop ssief!" So I want to see how she does at a crowded train station.

PATiENCE:

Earlier today I watched the 4-year-old flip through 318 pages (one at a time with consideration for each) of a German dictionary. Then she got to the start of the "H" section and said, "Ah . . . H!"

Her name begins with H.

NUTCRAPPER:

That moment you get paged to the backstage area because your 4-year-old had "a ax-dent" in her mouse costume.

ONE-MAN BAND:

Me (after hearing my daughter cough and fart at the same time): *Did you just cough and toot simultaneously?*

6-year-old: *Why?*

Me: *That's pretty impressive.*

6-year-old: *It was a duet.*

SCHOOL SHOOTiNG:

6-year-old: *Mama, why does God let people die?*

Me: *That's a good question. I don't know the answer.*

6-year-old: *I understand old people, but why childwen?*

Me: *(after a long pause) Maybe He wanted them back in heaven with Him. Maybe He wanted them close to Him.*

6-year-old: *So he doesn't want ME?*

This is a conversation no one ever should have to have.

SANTA'S ACCESS:

6-year-old: *Can Santa see me when I'm naked?*

(pause)

Me: *Let's think about that. He "sees you when you're sleeping and knows when you're awake. He knows if you've been bad or good," so I think you'll be fine. Just don't sleep naked.*

KNOWiNG ONE'S LiMiTATiONS:

4-year-old (grasping a wooden Christmas candle and its holder): *Mama, I ssink you ssould put dis somewhehwe out of weach because evewy time I pick it up, I bweak it.*

Me: *Well, then, maybe you shouldn't pick it up.*

4-year-old: *(pauses to consider . . . and then) Pwowwy best if you put it somewhewe high up.*

GETTiNG LUCKY:

Me (to 6-year-old): *How did I get you? How did I get so lucky?*

6-year-old: *God gave me to you.*

Me (to 4-year-old): *How did I get YOU?*

4-year-old: *Fwom youw bewwy. Ohw youw butt.*

Both (at least slightly) correct.

EARLY MORNINGS:

"I ssink tomowwohw I will sweep in" said no 4-year-old ever.

PEEP SHOW:

4-year-old (pointing to her breasts): *Why awe dese pawt of my pwivacy?*

Husband: *Because someday they'll get big like Mommy's, and people will want to see them.*

4-year-old: *Mommy, I see youws?*

Me: *No. We don't need to do that at the dinner table.*

Husband (to 4-year-old): *Tell her you'll give her a nickel.*

Now I'm wondering what to do with the money.

PACT:

6-year-old: *Mommy, I hope I die befohwe you.*

Me: *What? Oh no! That would break my heart.*

6-year-old: *Can you die fwom a bwoken heawt?*

Me: *Yes, I suppose you can.*

6-year-old (without skipping a beat): *Good. We'll go togethehw.*

PARSING WORDS:

4-year-old (proudly pointing to arrangement of construction-paper shapes sticking to dining room wall): *And you said I counent gwue papew to duh waww.*

Me: *Actually, I said you can't. But I clearly meant you*
shouldn't.

DADDY DUTY:

Me (walking down into the basement to find Husband lying on couch, eyes closed, with small children sitting atop him, each playing with a different iThing): *Does anyone want to play a game?*

4-year-old: *We awe pwaying. It's a game cawwed Sweeping Daddy.*

CRAZY NEIGHBOR LADY:

4-year-old: *Mama, dance wif me.*

Me (looking out the window at the twilight-colored empty sidewalk): *Why not?*

So we dance. And we dance. And I am very silly because I want the 4-year-old to learn the value of dancing "like no one's looking."

Then, as the cat-piano meowing music fades, I hear applause. I look out the window to the sidewalk now strewn with slack-jawed dog walkers. And I realize the 4-year-old is shorter than the windowsill.

MOMMY'S DAUGHTER:

Found in the 4-year-old's clutches after she fell asleep tonight: my dog-eared copy of Strunk and White's *Elements of Style*.

I'm proud and a little bit scared.

OF COURSE:

4-year-old (in her bed as I come in after work to say good night): *Mama, make ssuwe to tell Daddy to sweep wif me when he goes to bed.*

Me: *I'll tell him.*

4-year-old: *And Mama?*

Me: *Yes?*

4-year-old: *Tell him to weaw pants.*

SPARKLiNG COMPLEXiON:

That moment you realize someone used your makeup brush for an art project.

#glitter

TOO MUCH LOVE?:

New phrase coined by the 6-year-old: *I love you from the heawt of my bottom.*

SiX OF ONE, HALF DOZEN OF THE OTHER:

6-year-old: *I can count by fives.*

Me: *Go ahead.*

6-year-old: *Five, 10, 15, 20, 25, 30, 35, 40, 45 . . . 50!*

4-year-old: *I can count by twevves.*

Me: *Twelves? Wow. OK. Go ahead.*

4-year-old: *Twevve, and anuddew twevve, and anuddew twevve, and annudew twevve and aNUDDehw twevve!*

TIME TIPTOES ON:

I remember nibbling my daughters' plump, delicious baby feet. Toes like corn kernels, heels like marshmallows. Squiggly, wiggly baby feet. Moments ago I performed with laser-like precision the delicate task of trimming the 6-year-old's toenails, and I realized . . . Now they're just feet.

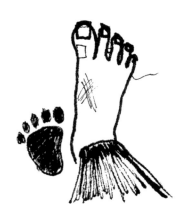

HARBiNGER:

Very rarely does good news follow these words:
"Mama, I has somssin to teww you."

COOKiE:

Me: *Please pick up your plate and put it in the sink.*

4-year-old (referring to her canine alter ego): *Cookie is a puppy. Cookie has paws. Puppies don't pick up pwates.*

Me: *Well, puppies don't wear pants, either, and YOU'RE wearing pants.*

That was a mistake.

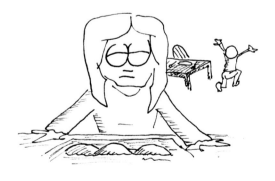

SURVEY SAYS:

4-year-old (while looking out the car window at an 18-wheeler with BUDWEISER scrawled on its side): *Is dat a wine twuck?*

Me: *No. It's a beer truck. Which do you think Mommy likes better? Beer or wine?*

4-year-old: *Is dat a twick quwestion?*

Me: *No. Why?*

6-year-old: *Because we know you love both.*

A NUMBERS GAME:

4-year-old (chirping as she clomps down two flights of stairs after bedtime): *Ninety-one, ninety-two, ninety-fwee, ninety-fohw . . .*

Me (sitting up on basement sofa, craning my neck and thinking): *I didn't know she could count that high.*

4-year-old: *Ninety-five, ninety-six, ninety-seven, ninety-eight . . .*

I rush to the bottom of the second flight in order to see the triumphant finale.

4-year-old: *Ninety-niiiiine . . . Fohwty*

THE "HARD" R:

4-year-old: *Mama, is I gwammawess?*

Me: *No. You have two grandmas. And a step-grandma. Why?*

4-year-old: *My fwiends say I is gwammawess.*

Me: *Why on earth would they say that?*

4-year-old: *'acause I weaw spawkiwy ssoes.*

#glamorous

BEDTIME ROUTINE:

I am currently watching 4-year-old "wind down" for bed by back-diving off the couch, landing on her head, then jumping up and yelling "I OK!"

All in her underwear because the nightgown gets in the way.

LEGAL EAGLES:

4-year-old: *What is a yaw?*

Me: *Hm. It's like a rule. But it's a rule that came from a bunch of politicians who voted on it and approved it. And if we disobey it, we could go to jail.*

4-year-old: *Oh. I get it. A yaw is yike "you have to wass youw hands, and you can't mehwwy youw sistuh."*

Me: *Exactly.*

HOUSE RULES:

4-year-old is dancing to music in her head. I watch for a few minutes, oooh-ing and aaah-ing with each pirouette. Then I hear the buzz of a new text message and slide my phone quietly closer.

6-year-old: *Excuse me. No electwonics in the theatuhw.*

ANOTHER BATH-TiME DELiGHT:

4-year-old (speaking conspiratorially to her sister in the bathtub): *Lessee if I can make a big cwap undew duh watew.*

Me (dropping laundry mid-fold and rushing from bedroom to bathroom): *Noooooo!!!*

Both girls look up, startled, and 4-year-old yanks her hands out of the water and raises them.

Me: *Oh. You said big CLAP.*

AND ONE MORE BATH-TiME DELiGHT:

6-year-old (after letting rip a noisy underwater fart): *Oops! I tooted.*

4-year-old: *Do it again! We can have a bubbew baf!*

Not one of their better ideas.

ANOTHER "POTTY" WORD:

6-year-old: *Tomowwow is Easter and that means we can say the A-word.*

Me: *What??? We don't say the A-word.*

6-year-old: *But tomowwohw we can.*

Then she exaggeratedly mouths, "Aaaaaaaaah-lehhhhhhh-luuuuuuuu-iaaaaaaaa."

DECISION-MAKING:

I am always amused when the 4-year-old and 6-year-old treat eeny, meeny, miney, and mo with the same reverence as, say, the scientific method.

WORKAROUND:

4-year-old: *Dis sucks.*

Me: *What? We don't say that word!*

4-year-old: *Does we say "socks?"*

Me: *Yes. Of course.*

4-year-old: *Den dis socks!*

HUMiLiTY:

6-year-old: *What is humility?*

Me: *When you realize you're not the only one in the world and that you're not that important.*

6-year-old: *(long pause) I don't get it.*

#stillthecenteroftheworld

#mineatleast

MUSIC MAGIC:

We are sitting in a softly lit church for a charming wedding ceremony when the organist plays the introduction to a favorite hymn. Tossing aside my typical sotto voce approach, I turn to the 4-year-old and belt, "Joyful, joyful we adore thee" just as the light outside changes, filling the room with warmth. The 4-year-old's eyes widen, and she puts her hand on my cheek to turn my head toward the golden glow of the stained glass windows. Then she whispers, "Mama, you woke up duh sun."

THE TRUTH ABOUT FARTS:

Me (after 6-year-old farts, looks around, sees she's been noticed and winces): *Don't worry. Sometimes toots just sneak out.*

6-year-old: *I know. And they always do it behind your back.*

Indeed.

MAIS OUI:

6-year-old: *Mama, I know how to French kiss.*

Me: *What???*

6-year-old: *Let me show you.*

I pause and then lean down, offering a pucker.

6-year-old kisses one cheek and then the other.

Of course. That IS how they kiss in France.

PARENTiNG:

Seeing something foreign on the floor, picking it up, smelling it . . . and then taking a bite. Last week it was a gumball on the hard wood. Tonight I found a small, round, brown clump hanging on the bottom of the 4-year-old's night shirt.

The 4-year-old said it was chocolate.

I DIDN'T bite.

BEAUTY:

6-year-old (emerging from room with confidence-inspiring sequined headband framing her face): *I don't mean to brag, but I'm beautiful.*

Immediately the responses spin Wheel of Fortune-like through my mind:

(All people are beautiful because God made us that way.

Being beautiful on the inside is more important than the outside.

Of course you are, but, then, I'm your mother, so you could have seven eyes, 12 arms, and one tooth, and I'd think you were beautiful.

Geez! Don't say that out loud. People will hate you!)

And then . . .

Me: *Yes, you are.*

Because someone, somewhere, someday will make her think she isn't.

WORDS THAT SHOULD MAKE A MOM WARY:

4-year-old: *Mama, don't come downstaiws.*

Me: *Why?*

4-year-old: *Nussin'.*

Me: *What is going on down there?*

4-year-old: *Nussin'! Nussin' fohw you to see.*

#thewritingsonthewall

#literally

BETTER THAN CABLE:

Husband (watching daughters sing and dance to Christmas tunes while wearing a combination of swimsuits, tutus and jammies): *Sometimes I feel like I'm living in a Wes Anderson film.*

I hope it's the Tenenbaum one.

MOTHER'S DAY:

4-year-old: *Today is Muddah's Day. Dat means mamas haf to do evewyfing. So pwease get me some socks.*

TRUTH:

Me: *What is the most important thing parents do?*

7-year-old: *Parents have a great responsibility to raise their children well.*

(I nod and contemplate the responsibility and then turn to smaller child.)

4-year-old: *Dem wipe deihw butts!*

EVEN MORE BATH-TiME DELiGHTS:

Me (walking into "bath time" and finding 4-year-old standing above 7-year-old, squirting water from an ancient shampoo bottle clutched with both hands just below her belly button): *WHAT ARE YOU DOING?*

4-year-old: *I peeping on my sistah!*

Me: *Sit down! Why on earth would you do that?*

7-year-old: *I taught her.*

There are no words. Except for maybe "solo baths from now on."

iNFLECTiON:

I have managed to turn a fairly innocuous word into a threat.

"GIIIIIRRRRRRLLLLLS!"

Stops 'em in their tracks every time.

(Knock wood.)

SYNONYMS:

4-year-old: *I know what a booty is.*

Me: *You do, huh? Tell me.*

4-year-old: *It's a tweasuwe . . . and youw butt.*

ANOTHER GUT PUNCH:

4-year-old: *Mama, what's dat song you'we singing?*

Me: *It's called "'Til There Was You."*

4-year-old: *What it's about?*

Me: *A young woman who thought she'd never find love, but then she found love. I like it because it says dreams can come true. And you should never give up. Do you like it?*

4-year-old (without skipping a beat): *No.*

FiRE SAFETY:

That moment when you're working from home (because you have a new sitter) and all the smoke detectors go off due to a fire in the oven, so the 4-year-old runs into the front yard, yelling "Caww 9-1-1" while the 7-year-old stops, drops and rolls.

ANOTHER AWKWARD STUFFED ANIMAL NAME:

4-year-old has a new stuffed turtle.

Nickname is "Tuwdy."

That's "Terdy" for those playing at home.

I. Can. Not.

BACKTRACKiNG:

4-year-old (on a city bus): *Why does you need to sit next to me?*

Me: *Because I'm your mother, and I want to keep you safe.*

4-year-old: *I wiss I had anudduh mudduh.*

Me: *That was not a kind thing to say.*

(Silence for eight minutes.)

4-year-old: *'Membuw when I said dat ssing about anudduh mudduh? I was being sawcastic.*

CLASSIFICATION:

4-year-old: *Is a awtichoke a amimal?*

Me: *No. It's a plant.*

4-year-old: *Den why does it have a heawt?*

Indeed. Especially when so many humans DON'T.

ALWAYS THINKING OF OTHERS:

7-year-old: *I wish Uncle Andy would get married.*

Me: *Why? Are you worried he might be lonely? Maybe finding someone to love would make him happier?*

7-year-old: *No. I want to be a flower girl.*

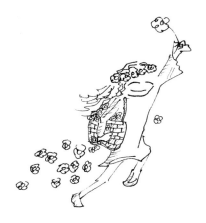

MORE WHITE LIES:

7-year-old (to little sister, whose favorite stuffed animal is a pig and whose favorite food happens to be ham, as she eats her lunch): *Do you know what ham really is?*

4-year-old shakes head and keeps chewing.

7-year-old: *It's PIG. You're eating PIG!*

4-year-old spits chewed ham into her hands.

Me: *THIS is TURKEY ham. Not pig ham.*

4-year-old pops ham back into mouth, gives sister triumphant smile, and resumes chewing.

BRIGHT SPOTS:

Me (to 4-year-old): *You are the light of my life.*

4-year-old: *Awwwwww . . .*

Me: *What? Does that make you happy?*

4-year-old: *No. You just need to weaw sungwasses.*

(I said the same thing to the 7-year-old, who replied, "I know.")

STOPPED SHORT:

Me (tucking in 7-year-old): *You're a smart, smart, funny, funny girl. And you're kind and generous, and I lov- - -*

7-year-old: *Can I just go to bed?*

(Sound of air slowly escaping balloon . . .)

iNTUiTiON:

4-year-old: *Can I pway wif youw pwetty scawves?*

Me: *We'll talk about it after lunch.*

4-year-old (beaming): *Dat means you'we going to say "yes."*

4-year-old (hours later at a street fest): *Can I have some doughnuts?*

Me: *We'll talk about it after dinner.*

4-year-old (sighing): *Dat means you'we going to say "no."*

She was right on both counts.

ANOTHER CLUE YOU'RE A PARENT:

Holding out your hand to take the bubble gum chewed by someone else. And if you're a lazy parent and don't want to find the nearest garbage can or napkin or scrap of paper, you put that gum right in your mouth.

BATH-TIME FOR COOKIE:

Me (to girls after a day of swimming, sweating, and screening the sun): *OK. Time for a bath.*

4-year-old (channeling canine alter ego): *Cookie is a dog. Dogs take bafs by yicking demsewves.*

4-year-old starts licking her arm.

I am now waiting for the day when the 4-year-old sees an actual dog lick itself where dogs really like to lick.

WISHFUL THINKING:

7-year-old: *Why does life have to be so hard?*

Me: *What's hard about it?*

7-year-old: *I have tangly hair, and I don't know all the answers in math.*

Me: *If you knew all the answers, you'd have nothing to learn. And life might get a little boring, right?*

7-year-old: *I'd like to try it for a day.*

SWIMMING:

4-year-old (after getting out of the pool): *Dat watuh was so cohd, duh fuhw on my yegs gwohwed.*

MORE "POTTY" WORDS:

7-year-old: *I know someone who said the "h" word.*

Me: *Oh. "Hate?" Yeah. We don't say that.*

7-year-old: *And someone said the "i" word.*

Me: *Idiot? Again . . . not in our vocabulary.*

7-year-old: *And the "j" word, too.*

Me: *"J" word? . . . Remind me of that.*

7-year-old mouths the word "jerk."

7-year-old: *But worst was the "s-h" word.*

Me (eyes widening): *Wait. What??*
Someone said the "s-h" word?

7-year-old (whispering): *Yes.*
Someone said "shut up."

TOO MUCH:

7-year-old (bursting into tears): *I don't want my life to go on.*

Me: *What? Why? What happened?*

(7-year-old sobs.)

Me: *Come sit with me. Are you hurt?*

(More sobs.)

Me: *Did someone say something mean?*

(More sobs.)

Me: *(pauses to think and then) Are you scared about the first day of school?*

(Silence.)

(continued on next page)

Me (struggling to catch my breath as a flood of long-forgotten fears slams into my chest): *I'll be there with you.*

7-year-old: *Will you stay all day?*

Me: *Yes.*

Having children is like reliving every joy and pain of early life. It's almost too much.

EVEN MORE CLEANING:

I am watching daughters play "cleaning lady" in our hotel room and wondering why this doesn't happen at home.

HOW BAD CAN iT BE?:

7-year-old: *Does God see me naked?*

Me: *No. Just your soul.*

7-year-old: *Not my "privates?"*

Me: *Just what's on the inside.*

7-year-old: *Oh. So He can read my thoughts?*

Me: *Yes.*

7-year-old: *(pauses before whispering) Uh oh.*

TAKING THE LONG VIEW:

4-year-old (upon finding a key chain with a picture of Husband and me): *Oh good. Now I'ww have a way of wemembewing you when you'we dead.*

(Stunned silence.)

SAY WHAT?:

Me (after several warnings to the screaming people in the back seat of the car): *That. Is. Enough. Do you want a spanking?*

(Silence.)

7-year-old: *What's a spanking?*

Me: *That's when a mom or dad hits your bottom because you misbehaved.*

7-year-old: *But how does hitting a bottom stop someone from misbehaving?*

Me: *It makes you think twice about doing it again. So it's like a warning.*

7-year-old: *Well, that's not going to work. I never remember what you say.*

DON'T QUIT YOUR DAY JOB:

7-year-old: *How much do professional football players make? Like 1,000 dollars?*

Me: *Some make more than a million.*

7-year-old: *WHO?*

Me: *Quarterbacks . . . because they need to call plays, complete passes, make handoffs, and sometimes run.*

7-year-old: *That sounds pretty easy . . . if you're not afraid of the ball.*

(pause)

7-year-old: *I'm afraid of the ball.*

Me: *Me, too.*

CiTY KiD:

7-year-old (emerging from an outhouse at a state park where her family spent the weekend in a cabin): *Remind me to forget this ever happened.*

THIS IS NOT GOING TO BE EASY:

7-year-old: *Can I read a bedtime story to my sister tonight?*

Me: *"May" you?*

7-year-old (blinking): **Can* I?*

Me: *"Can" means "Are you able?" "May" means "Do you have permission?"*

7-year-old (without skipping a beat): *May I have permission to say "can?"*

ETiQUETTE:

Me (as 5-year-old tries to shove a lollipop in her daddy's face): *Whoa . . . Settle down. That's inappropriate.*

5-year-old: *You know what ewse is inapwopwiate?*

Me: *What?*

5-year-old: *Putting youw hands in youw butt.*

Indeed.

NATURE OR NURTURE (AGAIN)?:

5-year-old (dragging out box of Husband's childhood Matchbox finery): *Daddy, yet's pway caws.*

Husband (eyes lighting up as he awkwardly sits on the floor): *OK!*

5-year-old: *Hewe's duh mommy caw, hewe's duh daddy caw, and dese two awe babies.*

Husband (sighing): *Of course.*

LOVE iS LOVE, BUT GROSS iS BETTER:

Me: *Today is a very special day. A new law lets boys marry boys and girls marry girls.*

7-year-old (falling to the floor in dramatic fashion): *What??? Why would boys marry boys?*

5-year-old (following suit): *Whyyyyyy? Getting maywwied is gwoss!*

7-year-old: *BOYS are gross!*

Husband: *Maybe they're too young for this discussion.*

SELF SOOTHING:

I have never been a mom who could watch her baby/
toddler/5- or 7-year-old fall and not react. I know
I should tell them "You're OK," but when I hear a
thud or see some blood, I go into Mother Hen mode,
grabbing them, hoisting them into a big bear hug, and
rubbing circles between their shoulder blades. I always
thought it calmed them. Until today.

**Me (hearing a crash from the living room and starting
the sprint toward the noise):** *Are you OK???*

**5-year-old (emerging from around the corner with
head hanging low):** *I OK . . .*

(5-year-old then raises her arms for the inevitable lift,
and I, who am now sweating, grab her and swing her up

(continued on next page)

for the love. About 45 seconds pass with the 5-year-old hanging limp, head on my shoulder, arms and legs dangling, while I soothe and snuggle. And then:)

5-year-old: *Do you feel better now?*

#cuethetears

#nothers

#mine

MATH:

5-year-old: *What's 'finity pwus 'finity?*

7-year-old: *Twofinity.*

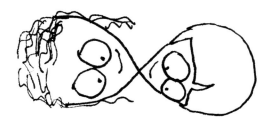

CORPORATE KIDS:

The 5-year-old and 7-year-old have started referring to themselves as "Dan" and "Bob."

I want to ask them if they work in accounting.

NOT JUST SUGAR AND SPiCE:

Husband (after a particularly dramatic morning with the 7-year-old): *I think she might have emotional issues.*

Me (to myself): *I think she's a girl.*

WHEAT, PLEASE:

As the family sits down to eat the homemade, kid-decorated birthday cupcakes, both girls wiggle with excitement. They lunge toward the unassuming pastries and are quiet, mouths full, for the first time all day. Then the quiet goes from victory to panic as both get up and run toward the garbage, spitting out sprinkles along the way.

5-year-old: *I yike GWUTEN!*

Husband and I laugh-weep into our own miserable cupcakes.

Me (whispering): *She's right. These are terrible.*

Husband (wiping his eyes): *Happy birthday.*

JUST LIKE HER FATHER:

7-year-old (while in a hot tub on holiday with the kids of our best friends): *What we have are nipples. When they get big, like my mom's, they're called boobs.*

5-year-olds (shouting): *Nipples? Boobs? Hahahahahaha!*

Me (surprising them from around the corner): *Actually, ladies, they're called breasts.*

(Silence.)

7-year-old: *I prefer "boobs."*

A CASE FOR SLEEVES:

5-year-old: *Evewyone has fwee pwivate pawts.*

Me: *Three? (wracking my brain) That sounds about right. But tell me: What are the three?*

5-year-old: *Duh butt, duh boobs, and duh awmpits.*

Me: *Armpits?*

5-year-old: *Yes. But ohn-wy if dey have haiw.*

PiONEER PAST:

Me: *When I grew up we didn't have bottled water.*

5-year-old: *Did you have sippy cups?*

7-year-old: *Did you have cups?*

5-year-old: *Did you have cup hohdehws?*

7-year-old: *Did you have cars?*

5-year-old: *Did you have wagons?*

Me: *We had water fountains.*

#attheoutposts

#withtroughsforthehorses

OUCH:

5-year-old: *You know I love Daddy mohwe.*

Me: *Yes, I know.*

5-year-old: *Dat's 'acause I've towhd you 'afohwe.*

Me: *Yes, you have.*

7-year-old: *I have four words for you, Mama. Cry out the pain.*

LiFE LESSONS:

5-year-old (worried about going to school after long weekend): *What if aww my fwiends yeahwned somefin', and I dinnent?*

Me: *What were you hoping to learn?*

5-year-old: *How to buiwd a human.*

SO MUCH FOR "LESS IS MORE":

7-year-old: *Why don't you wear makeup?*

Me: *I DO wear makeup.*

7-year-old: *Why aren't you wearing it now?*

Me: *I AM wearing it now.*

7-year-old: *Oh.*

FASHION FOOTWEAR:

That moment when, after bundling kids up to their eyeballs, strapping them into car seats, and speeding down snowy streets toward the elementary school basketball game, you look down and realize you're wearing your slippers.

BEHIND EVERY MAN:

5-year-old (after long bath): *Why does God make pwune-y toes?*

Me: *I don't think God makes your toes prune-y. I think the water is responsible.*

5-year-old: *I ssink Mrs. God is in chawge of toes.*

UH-OH:

5-year-old: *I need a by-buhw.*

Me: *Do you know what a Bible is?*

5-year-old: *It's a book of faiwytaywes about God.*

FAIL-SAFE:

Husband: *I think we should have a game night once a week.*

Me: *Hmmm. I guess the girls are old enough now. It won't be so frustrating.*

Husband: *Frustrating for them or for you?*

Me: *(guilty silence)*

Husband: *You know, you could let them win once in a while.*

Me: *It's important for them to learn to fail in a safe environment.*

(Husband shakes his head and laughs sadly.)

FUTURE URCHiN:

5-year-old (after a difficult bedtime drill): *I wiss I was a stweet giwl.*

Me: *How would you stay warm?*

5-year-old: *I wounent.*

Me: *Who would feed you when your tummy rumbled?*

5-year-old: *No one.*

Me: *Who would kiss you when you had a boo-boo?*

5-year-old: *No one. Dat's duh point.*

Me (to myself): *I'll miss you.*

PRIORITIES:

7-year-old (working the charm at bedtime): *May I pleathe have thum water?*

Me: *Um. Of course. But can you say pleasssse?*

7-year-old: *What'th wrong with pleathe?*

Me: *It makes you sound like a little girl.*

7-year-old: *I AM a little girl.*

Me: *OK.* (starting the trek down to the kitchen) *But you want to be taken seriously.*

7-year-old (shouting after her):
I'd really rather be cute.

CALL OF THE WILD:

Me (walking into my bedroom and seeing two naked girls crawling on the floor): *What are you doing???*

5-year-old: *We'we being animaws.*

Me: *Where are your clothes???*

7-year-old: *Animals don't wear clothes.*

#cantarguewiththelogic

#butstillfinditalittlecreepy

BiTiNG BACK LAUGHTER:

For years Husband and I have referred to the unmentionables in one's nose as "bears in the cave." Tonight this happened:

Me (entering room for bedtime books and seeing 5-year-old with finger up her nose): *What are you doing?*

5-year-old: *I'm hunting for beaws.*

EXTRA CREDIT:

7-year-old: *Why do some kids leave class to go to the tutor?*

5-year-old (exploding with laughter): *'Acause dey hafta toot!*

(I stay quiet because there's no point messing with perfection.)

LATE FOR THE GAME AGAIN:

The 7-year-old, when asked to hurry, accelerates from meander to mosey.

HOW DEEP iS MY LOVE?:

Giddy about finally having trained the 5-year-old to take showers, I walk into the bathroom to offer help and find said 5-year-old rinsing her armpits by striking Travolta-like *Saturday Night Fever* poses under the stream of water. I turn away before witnessing the way she chooses to rinse her bottom.

STAYING OUT OF THE SEWER:

5-year-old: *Mama, when we dwain duh bafftub, does it go into duh sewuhw?*

Me: *Yes.*

5-year-old: *When we fwuss duh toi-yet does it go into duh sewuhw?*

Me: *Yes.*

5-year-old: *So it's fine to go potty in duh bafftub.*

Me (desperately wanting to be sarcastic but knowing the perils): *No.*

THE LADIES ROOM:

5-year-old (bursting into the bathroom where I am in a state of undress): *It's OK, Mama. I'm ayyowwed to see youw pwivacy 'acause we'we bof yadies.*

TiPS FOR MAKING FRiENDS WHEN YOU'RE A KiD:

First kid: *Hi. I'm 5.*

Second kid: *I'm 5, too.*

Deal sealed.

NEXT BREAK: STAYCATION:

Me: *What was your favorite part of spring break? Was it the pool, the boat, the beach, or time with Baba and Boots?*

5-year-old: *(pauses, eyes rolling upward as she scans the mental replay of highlights of the week, before deciding with gusto) Duh gum.*

KiDS ARE LiTERAL:

5-year-old (after hearing radio announcer say the Blackhawks need to get a brief case of amnesia): *Why'd he say dat?*

Me: *Because they need to forget about their OT loss and concentrate on playing well NOW.*

5-year-old: *But if dey get um-neeza, dey won't uh-membehw how to pway hockey.*

EVERYONE GETS A TROPHY:

On the back of a tattered children's menu, a dozen fiercely scrawled tic-tac-toe games show evidence of the competitive nature of mother and daughter. I am proud. Then the 7-year-old tallies the score and adds two lines at the bottom of the page.

Winner: _____ and

Tryer: _____ .

#whathappenedtothelosers?

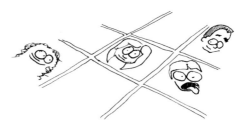

ACKNOWLEDGMENTS:

Thanks to Steve Alexander, Diane Montiel, and Bonnie Hayskar for helping me dip my toe into the murky waters of publishing. I had no idea. Thanks to Brooke Warner, Tabitha Lahr, and Lauren Wise for teaching me to swim those waters and emerge with a book I love.

So many friends, family, and colleagues provided much-needed feedback and encouragement during the writing process. Thanks to Marya, Matt, Alicia, Danialle, Cochran, Kogan, Tanja, Arek, Ed, and the unbelievable JBP.

Thanks also to the countless other players in our lives who helped make this book happen: babysitters Kate, Rebekah, and Sophia, cousins Carolyn and Mad, Uncle Tomato, my families at Northwestern and WGN, the women of AWJ-Chicago, the teachers and professors at WHS, Yale, and Medill, the moms and dads of St. Ben's, Bell and Waters, the ladies of the Cookie Bake, the unicorn collection that is The Manor, and the incomparable community of Woodstock, Illinois.

I dedicated this book to my husband, my daughters, and my parents, but it bears repeating: I love them "more than the twinkles in the stars."

ABOUT THE AUTHOR:

Anne Johnsos is an award-winning journalist determined to document the "oofs" and "acks" of parenting. Let's face it: Kids inhabit an innocent kind of ass-hattery as they learn language and decorum. After years of recording the ways her kids interpreted the world, Anne realized their words needed pictures, so she reconnected with a fellow former performer from Yale who happens to be an illustrator, and *Potty-Mouthed* was born.

Author photo © Carolyn Rikje

ABOUT THE iLLUSTRATOR:

John Britton is a new dad illustrating Anne's playlets on any piece of paper he can find without his son's bite marks or his daughter's drool. He's a published illustrator and an award-winning animator who got sidetracked by the law (as a copyright and trademark attorney and professor) but found his way back to his pen in the *Potty-Mouthed* series. He also prefers to remain anonymous just in case no one likes the book.

ABOUT SPARKPRESS:

SparkPress is an independent, hybrid imprint focused on merging the best of the traditional publishing model with new and innovative strategies. We deliver high-quality, entertaining, and engaging content that enhances readers' lives. We are proud to bring to market a list of *New York Times* best-selling, award-winning, and debut authors who represent a wide array of genres, as well as our established, industry-wide reputation for creative, results-driven success in working with authors. SparkPress, a BookSparks imprint, is a division of SparkPoint Studio LLC.

Learn more at GoSparkPress.com